THE MIRACLES OF JESUS

A 30-DAY DEVOTIONAL

BY TONY MYLES AND SETH MCCOY

Kansas City, Missouri

Copyright 2011 by Youthfront and Barefoot Ministries®

ISBN 978-0-8341-5051-5

Printed in the United States of America

Editing: Jen Howver and Michael Novelli
Interior Design: Kevin Parker
Cover Design: Arthur Cherry

Unless otherwise indicated, all Scripture quotations are taken from the Holy Bible, New Living Translation, copyright 1996. Used by permission of Tyndale House Publishers, Inc., Wheaton, Illinois 60189. All rights reserved.

The *Holy Bible, New International Version*® (NIV®). Copyright © 1973, 1978, 1984 by International Bible Society. Used by permission of Zondervan Publishing House. All rights reserved.

Library of Congress Control Number: 2010942104

9 8 7 6 5 4 3 2 1

INTRODUCTION

WELCOME TO A THIRTY-DAY JOURNEY THROUGH THE MIRACLES OF JESUS.

In everyday conversations we use the word "miracle" to describe things that are incredible, unbelievable, or highly unlikely.

"That shot from half-court was a miracle…"

"It would take a miracle for me to pass that test…"

"It's a miracle that you didn't get grounded!"

When we use the word "miracle" for so many of our daily experiences, the power of the concept gets diluted. It becomes hard to grasp how huge the miracles in the Bible really were. Jesus performed miracles as a sign—to show people the power of God (and that he actually *was* God). The miracles of Jesus also serve as a pathway for us to learn more about this God who created us, and to deepen our relationship with him.

The miracles Jesus performed reveal the true nature of God. Along this journey we will help you see the Father, as we look at Jesus. This devotional will awaken you to God's love and care for you, and the fullness of life that he desires for us all. When we think of life, we sometimes focus on the eternal life Jesus brings, but there's much more to his offer of life. In these pages, you'll discover the God that people experienced in these miracle stories, and if you look closely, you'll find abundant life in Jesus today.

This devotional focuses on the miracles of healing in Jesus ministry. You may have heard some of the stories—the blind seeing again, the deaf hearing again, lame people walking, lepers made clean, and even dead people coming back to life. Whether you've heard these stories or not, as you spend time reflecting on them here, you'll discover that the common thread between all the stories is the life and wholeness people found in Jesus. And you'll also find that no matter where you are in life, or what you're dealing with, you can also find life and wholeness in Jesus.

The miracles you'll read about here are from the four books in the Bible called the "Gospels." The word gospel means "good news" or message. In fact, the word originated in Rome; any time a new emperor took power, they would send messengers all over the Roman Empire to proclaim the "good news" of the peace and prosperity the new emperor would bring. These Gospels are very much like that. They tell a story of a new King, but a king unlike the world has ever seen. Matthew, Mark, Luke, and John each tell the story of the new King from their own viewpoint, and each day you will find God revealing himself to you through Jesus' miracles.

MAKING THE MOST OF THIS DEVOTIONAL

Here are a few tips to help you dive into the devotional so you can get the most out of it:

- Invite the Holy Spirit to speak to you using the words of the prayer included each day, or use your own words.

- If you miss a day don't feel guilty or give up; just pick up where you left off. God is not taking attendance.

- If you like your version of the Bible better than the one we've used, go ahead and use it.

- Remember this time is not about an agenda or about meeting anyone's expectations. It's a personal journey, and you should walk at your own pace as you seek to draw closer to God.

THE ELEMENTS OF THIS DEVOTIONAL

Every day has five different opportunities to help you experience the story:

PRAYER

A space for you to invite God's Spirit to speak to you through the Scriptures.

READING

A reading from one of the Gospels that explores one of Jesus' revealing miracles.

RESPONSE

A section for you to write out your thoughts or questions about the story.

INSIGHT

Thoughts and ideas from history that may help unfold more of the story through the eyes of the people who first experienced it.

REFLECTION

Exercises that will help you explore how these ideas might shape your heart and life.

Imagine what God could do in you as you spend the next thirty days walking with Jesus through his revealing miracles. Watch as God reveals his love for you through the healing miracles Jesus performed. May this journey bring you closer to the one who brings life, healing, and wholeness.

DAY 1

PREPARE TO WITNESS THE MIRACLES OF JESUS

PRAYER

Jesus, I am on this journey to find wholeness
and life in you.
Take these weeks and shape my life around your life.
Be my teacher and guide.

Take a few minutes of silence. In your own words, ask God to meet you here.

READING

In those days John the Baptist came to the Judean wilderness and began preaching. His message was, "Repent of your sins and turn to God, for the Kingdom of Heaven is near." The prophet Isaiah was speaking about John when he said, "He is a voice shouting in the wilderness, 'Prepare the way for the Lord's coming! Clear the road for him!'"
—MATTHEW 3:1-3

After reading those verses, what are your first impressions? How would you have responded to John the Baptist's message? Write down anything that comes to your mind about the passage.

INSIGHT

Each of the Gospels records an event in history—the story of the life and ministry of Jesus, a Jewish man from Nazareth, who lived in Israel in the first century. In the writer's eyes this was the biggest event in world history, but especially in Jewish history.

Ancient prophecy played a large part in how first century Jewish people saw life. One of the Jewish prophets foretold that there would be a person like the great prophet Elijah to prepare the way for the Messiah. John the Baptist fulfilled this role, challenging people to repent from their sins so that they would be prepared to receive the Messiah when he came. Jesus described his mission when He read from Isaiah in the synagogue in his hometown:

> "The Spirit of the Lord is upon me, for he has anointed me to bring Good News to the poor. He has sent me to proclaim that captives will be released, that the blind will see, that the oppressed will be set free, and that the time of the Lord's favor has come."

> He rolled up the scroll, handed it back to the attendant, and sat down. All eyes in the synagogue looked at him intently. Then he began to speak to them. "The Scripture you've just heard has been fulfilled this very day!"
> —Luke 4:18-20

As we hear his words it becomes clear that miracles will be a central part of his ministry. Jesus used miracles to reveal the one true God, and through the Scriptures, you have the opportunity to see that God for yourself.

As you prepare yourself to witness the miracles of Jesus, what are you hoping you'll discover through this journey?

In what areas of your life are you hoping to find life, healing, and wholeness?

Take a few minutes to write a letter to God, expressing what you hope to learn from Jesus' miracles. Ask for wisdom to apply the lessons to your own life.

DAY 2

GOD REVEALED THROUGH MATTHEW

PRAYER

God, you are the Word.
Open my eyes to the person behind this story.
Help me to see these miracles of Jesus from
Matthew's eyes, and show me what I can learn from
this tax collector.

Take a few minutes of silence. In your own words, ask God to meet you here.

READING

As Jesus was walking along, he saw a man named Matthew sitting at his tax collector's booth. "Follow me and be my disciple," Jesus said to him. So Matthew got up and followed him.

Later, Matthew invited Jesus and his disciples to his home as dinner guests, along with many tax collectors and other disreputable sinners.

—MATTHEW 9:9-10

RESPONSE

After reading those verses, what are your first impressions? What do you imagine it was like to be at that dinner party? Write down anything that comes to your mind about this passage.

INSIGHT

We find Matthew sitting at his tax collector's booth. It was his job to collect the Roman taxes from his fellow Jewish people. To most Jewish people of his day, this was seen as an act of betrayal, because they viewed the Romans as the godless occupying forces, and Matthew was helping them collect money to fund the occupation and support Rome. Most tax collectors in Israel would also add their own taxes, sometimes even doubling them. It was possible for a Jewish man to pay 75 percent of his income in taxes. These tax collectors were disliked because they stole from their own people, and helped the Romans steal from them.

The Jewish people recognized Jesus as a "rabbi," or teacher. Rabbis would invite a special group of students to follow them and learn how to be a rabbi. It was the dream of every Jewish boy to be called to follow a rabbi and become his disciple; it was an honor to be called a disciple. This may explain why Matthew got up and followed Jesus so quickly. It made others question Jesus, however, since he chose one of society's most disliked people to follow him.

At first, this story may not seem like a miracle. But imagine the healing in Matthew's life—most people hated him, but Jesus loved him and brought him wholeness.

Matthew would later tell the story of the Messiah, Jesus of Nazareth. He experienced, first hand, a new life following Jesus. In the book of Matthew, we see the ways Jesus offers us new life and makes us new.

What do you think it would feel like to be hated by society, but then invited to follow the Son of God?

What would happen if you invited someone who is hated by everyone in your school to sit with you for lunch?

This week, take that challenge. Invite someone who is an outcast to sit with you during lunch. See what happens when you reach out in love to someone that everyone else sees as worthless.

DAY 3

JESUS FULFILLS THE PROPHECIES

PRAYER

God, you are called El-Shaddai.
You meet the needs of your people.

Help me notice the ways you meet my needs each day,
and equip me to meet the needs of those around me.

Take a few minutes of silence. In your own words, ask God to meet
you here.

READING

When Jesus arrived at Peter's house, Peter's mother-in-
law was sick in bed with a high fever. But when Jesus
touched her hand, the fever left her. Then she got up
and prepared a meal for him.

That evening many demon-possessed people were brought to Jesus. He cast out the evil spirits with a simple command, and he healed all the sick. This fulfilled the word of the Lord through the prophet Isaiah, who said, "He took our sicknesses and removed our diseases."

—Matthew 8:14-17

RESPONSE ⠿

After reading those verses what are your first impressions? What do you think it means that Jesus "fulfilled the word of the Lord through the prophet Isaiah?" Write down anything that comes to your mind about this passage.

INSIGHT

In this story, Matthew makes a connection between what Jesus did and what the prophets said the Messiah would do. In Matthew's gospel there are more Old Testament prophecies quoted than in any other gospel. Matthew wrote his gospel to help the Jewish people of his day see that Jesus was the Messiah—the promised one they had been waiting for.

In Matthew's day, the Jewish people were waiting expectantly for the promised Messiah. According to the prophets in the Old Testament, these were some of the things a Jewish person living in Jesus' day would expect to happen in the time of the Messiah:

- A remnant of Jewish people from all 12 tribes will return to the Land of Israel.

- All of the people of Israel will come back to, or follow, the Torah (the law).

- The holy Temple in Jerusalem will be rebuilt.

- Israel will live free among the nations, and will have no need to defend itself.

- The God of Israel will overthrow the tyrannical nations who are oppressing Israel.

- War and famine will end, and an era of peace and prosperity will come upon the Earth.

- This era will lead to supernatural events, including the bodily resurrection of the dead.

As you continue through the Gospels, remember that these were the things people expected of Jesus, if he really was the Messiah. He would restore Israel, punish the rebels, and set up his kingdom. As we keep reading in God's Word, Jesus continues to reveal the Kingdom of God, and he accomplishes all these things, but in ways people never expected.

REFLECTION ❖

Using your Bible, read these Scriptures about what God would do in the day of the Messiah. Write your thoughts about each passage.

Jeremiah 33:14-18

Isaiah 9:1-7

Isaiah 11:1-9

Zechariah 9:9-10

Imagine for a minute what it would have been like to be a Jewish child who heard these verses from the prophets. Then imagine what it would have been like to hear the stories of Jesus and the rumors that he was the fulfillment of these prophecies. Would you have been confused? Excited? Afraid? Write or draw your thoughts.

DAY 4

JESUS IS THE SON OF DAVID

PRAYER

Heavenly Father,
thank you for adopting me
into your holy family.

Deepen my faith through your word
and draw me closer to you.

Take a few minutes of silence. In your own words, ask God to meet
you here.

READING

After Jesus left the girl's home, two blind men followed
along behind him, shouting, "Son of David, have mercy
on us!"

They went right into the house where he was staying, and Jesus asked them, "Do you believe I can make you see?"

"Yes, Lord," they told him, "we do."

Then he touched their eyes and said, "Because of your faith, it will happen." Then their eyes were opened, and they could see! Jesus sternly warned them, "Don't tell anyone about this." But instead, they went out and spread his fame all over the region.
—Matthew 9:27-31

RESPONSE

After reading those verses, what are your first impressions? Why do you think Jesus told them not to tell anyone about being healed? Write down anything that comes to your mind about this passage.

INSIGHT ❖

The two men in this encounter with Jesus refer to him as the "Son of David." It seems strange that they'd call Jesus the Son of David, when we know in earlier verses he is the son of Mary and Joseph. However, in the Jewish Scriptures the phrase "Son of David" was sometimes used to refer to anyone from the line of David. In Matthew 1:20, Joseph is also called the son of David.

There is great significance that Jesus came from David's line. When these men identify Jesus as the Son of David, they were expressing faith that he was the Messiah. Jesus challenged them to go further. He wanted to know if they also believed that he could heal them. In response to both of their confessions of faith in him, he healed them.

REFLECTION ❖

What situations are you facing that require you to believe in and rely on the power of Jesus?

Take a moment and think about how much faith you need to get through a normal day? Do you feel weak or strong in faith?

How could you put yourself in situations that would require more faith?

Write out a prayer to God that expresses your reactions to these questions.

DAY 5

JESUS VS. DEMONS

PRAYER

God, you are the Lord Most High, El-Elyon.
I am grateful for your power over evil.

Protect me today and
strengthen me to stand firm in you.

Take a few minutes of silence. In your own words, ask God to meet
you here.

READING

When they left, a demon-possessed man who couldn't
speak was brought to Jesus. So Jesus cast out the
demon, and then the man began to speak. The crowds
were amazed. "Nothing like this has ever happened in
Israel!" they exclaimed.

But the Pharisees said, "He can cast out demons
because he is empowered by the prince of demons."
—MATTHEW 9:32-34

After reading those verses, what are your first impressions? Why do you think the Pharisees thought Jesus was "empowered by the prince of demons?" Write down anything that comes to your mind about this passage.

INSIGHT

It's not unusual in our culture to make a distinction between the world of the physical and the world of the spiritual. If we said an illness was being caused by a demon we would sound crazy to everyone around us. When Jesus walked the earth there was no distinction. We even hear the disciples ask Jesus "who sinned?" when they came in contact with a blind man—wondering which of the parents was to blame for the blindness (John 9:1). Jesus was the only one who could actually see what was really happening in the world. From the stories of demon possession that we see in the gospels, it would seem that not even the religious leaders had any power over the demons.

As we see in this story, sometimes demons influence, and even possess people. But we notice that the people who are supposed to know God and recognize his work claim that Jesus is empowered by the prince of demons. They don't even see that Jesus is more powerful than demons because he *is* God.

How often do you think about the spirit world? How does it make you feel when you do think about it?

Take your Bible and read Ephesians 6:10-17. What pieces of armor do you need the most to help you stand strong against evil?

On another sheet of paper, draw or write out the pieces of armor that you need most, and hang them in a place where you'll see them everyday. When you see the picture or words, ask God to help you put that armor on each day.

DAY 6

JESUS BLURS THE LINES OF RACE

PRAYER

God, you are the Good Shepherd,
and you care for all your sheep.

Open my eyes to see people as you see them.
Open my heart to love them as you do.

Take a few minutes of silence. In your own words, ask God to meet you here.

READING

Then Jesus left Galilee and went north to the region of Tyre and Sidon. A Gentile woman who lived there came to him, pleading, "Have mercy on me, O Lord, Son of David! For my daughter is possessed by a demon that torments her severely."

But Jesus gave her no reply, not even a word. Then his disciples urged him to send her away. "Tell her to go away," they said. "She is bothering us with all her begging."

Then Jesus said to the woman, "I was sent only to help God's lost sheep—the people of Israel."

But she came and worshiped him, pleading again, "Lord, help me!"

Jesus responded, "It isn't right to take food from the children and throw it to the dogs."

She replied, "That's true, Lord, but even dogs are allowed to eat the scraps that fall beneath their masters' table."

"Dear woman," Jesus said to her, "your faith is great. Your request is granted." And her daughter was instantly healed.
—Matthew 15:21-28

RESPONSE

After reading those verses, what are your first impressions? Why do you think the woman continued to plea for Jesus' help, even though he ignored her and told her no? Write down anything that comes to your mind about this passage.

INSIGHT ⚫

In our world today we recognize several different nationalities. We might describe someone based on their race or nationality, referring to them as Italian, Irish, Hispanic, or Asian. Throughout history, however, race and nationality has been a sensitive topic.

When Jesus walked the earth, the Jewish perspective was that there were only two kinds of people—Jewish and not Jewish (Gentile). The Jewish people believed they were God's chosen people, destined to rule over the other nations of the world, and many Jewish people considered Gentiles to be unclean. In fact, a good Jewish man was not allowed to marry a Gentile, eat with them, or even talk with them.

What would it mean for a non-Jewish woman to approach a Jewish rabbi and ask him for something? Go back and reread this passage with that question in mind.

All through the Old Testament there is a promise that through Israel God will redeem and restore the whole world and all people. In the time of Jesus, God's people had forgotten that they were to be a light to the world. They had forgotten that God was the Lord of the whole earth and everything in it. A good portion of Paul's teaching to the churches in the New Testament centers around what it means for there to be reconciliation between Jewish and Gentile people, who now, because of the cross, make up one new family.

REFLECTION ⚫

In what ways can you see Jesus challenging his disciples to think differently about these ideas of race and superiority in this passage?

Read Revelation 7:9-12 and reflect on what heaven will look like. Imagine the kind of celebration that will take place as every tribe, tongue, and nation is gathered together under the loving rule of Jesus. Write out some thoughts about what that will look and feel like.

In the next few days, go to an ethnic restaurant to eat. While you're there:

- Eat some food that is new to you.

- Observe how the customers interact with the servers or environment.

- Try to learn some of the language. Ask your server how to say simple words such as "hello" and "thank you."

- After your meal, take a few minutes to write some thoughts about the experience. What did you notice about the people? How did it feel to try something new and different?

DAY 7

THE CROWDS FLOCK TO JESUS

PRAYER

Father, you are the One True God,
the one worthy of my praise.

I love you and thank you
for drawing me closer to you.

Take a few minutes of silence. In your own words, ask God to meet you here.

READING

Jesus returned to the Sea of Galilee and climbed a hill and sat down. A vast crowd brought to him people who were lame, blind, crippled, those who couldn't speak, and many others. They laid them before Jesus, and he healed them all. The crowd was amazed! Those who

35

hadn't been able to speak were talking, the crippled were made well, the lame were walking, and the blind could see again! And they praised the God of Israel.
—Matthew 15:29-31

RESPONSE

After reading those verses, what are your first impressions? How would you have reacted if you witnessed these healings? Write down anything that comes to your mind about this passage.

INSIGHT

You may have heard John 10:10 before, where Jesus says, "I have come that they may have life, and have it to the full" (NIV). Today's passage is an example and a symbol of the new and full life that Jesus was promising to all people who believed in him. People who had not been able to speak were now talking; blind people could see.

Similarly, when we embrace the power of Jesus in our own lives, he heals us, allowing us to speak of his love to others, and to see the amazing work God is doing around us. And much like the people who were healed by Jesus on that hillside, we will not be able to keep quiet about the wonderful things God is doing in our lives.

REFLECTION

What does this passage of Scripture tell you about God?

How have you seen God at work around you recently?

Share with someone this week about what God has done in your life. Talk about how you were "blind" before, and what you can actually "see" now.

DAY 8

FAITH TO MOVE MOUNTAINS

PRAYER

You are the Great I AM.
You spoke the world into creation, Lord,
and your power is infinite.

Pour your power into me,
deepen my faith,
help me to rely on you for everything I do.

Take a few minutes of silence. In your own words, ask God to meet you here.

At the foot of the mountain, a large crowd was waiting for them. A man came and knelt before Jesus and said, "Lord, have mercy on my son. He has seizures and suffers terribly. He often falls into the fire or into the water. So I brought him to your disciples, but they couldn't heal him."

Jesus said, "You faithless and corrupt people! How long must I be with you? How long must I put up with you? Bring the boy here to me." Then Jesus rebuked the demon in the boy, and it left him. From that moment the boy was well.

Afterward the disciples asked Jesus privately, "Why couldn't we cast out that demon?"

"You don't have enough faith," Jesus told them. "I tell you the truth, if you had faith even as small as a mustard seed, you could say to this mountain, 'Move from here to there,' and it would move. Nothing would be impossible."
—Matthew 17:14-20

RESPONSE

After reading those verses, what are your first impressions? If you were one of the disciples, how would you respond to Jesus' words about the mustard seed? Write down anything that comes to your mind about this passage.

INSIGHT

In this passage, Matthew is telling a story about the disciples, who were struggling to carry out the ministry Jesus was preparing them for. Earlier in the story, Jesus had sent them out with the ability to cast out demons and heal sickness, but soon after that, they were not able to perform these miracles for some reason. Jesus uses two important word pictures in calling them to grow in their faith and their ministry.

He first used the picture of a mustard seed. This was one of Jesus' favorite illustrations about faith and the Kingdom of God. A mustard seed is a tiny seed, but it grows into a six to ten-foot plant. Jesus is saying that in faith, you only need a little to produce something big.

Jesus also used the picture of a mountain being moved. It was common in Jewish thought that mountains, like trees, had roots, and that the roots of mountains went deep beneath the earth. To say, "move a mountain" was another to way to say something was impossible. The disciples, like all of us, needed to be reminded of the power they had through God if they just had faith.

REFLECTION

Take a moment to reflect on times or events in your life where you have seen God move a mountain—when he did what you thought was impossible. Make a list of these events in the space below.

DAY EIGHT: FAITH TO MOVE MOUNTAINS

What are you facing right now in your life that seems impossible to get through or overcome?

As you look at what you've written above, ask God to show you how he sees those problems.

Like the disciples, it's often difficult for us to have faith. Ask God to increase your faith in him. Write a prayer asking God for his help. Feel free to share your frustrations or thank him for what he has already done in your life.

If you want to experience moving mountains, write out your impossible problems (write each problem on a separate sheet of paper). Crumple up the papers and stack them into a mountain. Then, pray for each problem as you pick them up, one-by-one, and move the mountain to a new place.

DAY 9

GOD REVEALED THROUGH MARK

PRAYER

God, you are the Light of the world.
Open my eyes
to the truth you want me to learn
from this Gospel.

Give me wisdom to take this new knowledge
and use it in my life
to become more like my Savior.

Take a few minutes of silence. In your own words, ask God to meet you here.

READING

Before daybreak the next morning, Jesus got up and went out to an isolated place to pray. Later Simon and the others went out to find him. When they found him, they said, "Everyone is looking for you."

But Jesus replied, "We must go on to other towns as well, and I will preach to them, too. That is why I came." So he traveled throughout the region of Galilee, preaching in the synagogues and casting out demons.
—Mark 1:35-39

RESPONSE

After reading those verses, what are your first impressions? If you were there, what would you have said or done when you found Jesus praying? Write down anything that comes to your mind about this passage.

INSIGHT

In this passage, Simon and the others went to find Jesus, thinking that he'd be excited to know that everyone was looking for him. However, it's likely that he had retreated to pray for that very reason. He was constantly followed by people who hoped that he'd heal them, and he needed to reconnect to his Father to maintain his strength and stay focused on his mission. It's a reminder for us that Jesus relied on God's power to perform his miracles, and we need to rely on God for miracles in our lives as well.

REFLECTION

When you're feeling overwhelmed by people or demands on you, how do you retreat from it all to regain your strength? How does prayer tie into your life at these times?

How have you experienced prayer as a way to regain strength and focus on God?

Take a few minutes and go to "an isolated place" to be alone with God in prayer. Notice the sounds, the smells, the things you see around you. Spend a few minutes praying.

DAY 10

THE CONNECTION BETWEEN SIN AND SUFFERING

PRAYER

You are Immanuel—God with us.
Thank you for being with me always.

Help me to feel your presence,
and guide my steps to follow you
with all my heart.

Take a few minutes of silence. In your own words, ask God to meet you here.

When Jesus returned to Capernaum several days later, the news spread quickly that he was back home. Soon the house where he was staying was so packed with visitors that there was no more room, even outside the door. While he was preaching God's word to them, four men arrived carrying a paralyzed man on a mat. They couldn't bring him to Jesus because of the crowd, so they dug a hole through the roof above his head. Then they lowered the man on his mat, right down in front of Jesus. Seeing their faith, Jesus said to the paralyzed man, "My child, your sins are forgiven."

But some of the teachers of religious law who were sitting there thought to themselves, "What is he saying? This is blasphemy! Only God can forgive sins!"

Jesus knew immediately what they were thinking, so he asked them, "Why do you question this in your hearts? Is it easier to say to the paralyzed man 'Your sins are forgiven,' or 'Stand up, pick up your mat, and walk'? So I will prove to you that the Son of Man has the authority on earth to forgive sins." Then Jesus turned to the paralyzed man and said, "Stand up, pick up your mat, and go home!"

And the man jumped up, grabbed his mat, and walked out through the stunned onlookers. They were all amazed and praised God, exclaiming, "We've never seen anything like this before!"
—MARK 2:1-12

RESPONSE

After reading those verses, what are your first impressions? What would it feel like to be the paralyzed man whose friends lowered him into the room? Write down anything that comes to your mind about this passage.

The Jewish people often made a connection between sin and suffering. They assumed that if someone had a sickness or deformity it was because they, or a member of their family, had offended God. Imagine how terrifying it must have been for the paralyzed man as he lay before Jesus, wondering if he would be blamed for his condition. But Jesus first told the man his sins were forgiven. In fact, this trend is seen throughout Jesus' ministry. He makes a connection between the restoration he brings to our bodies (healing), and the restoration he brings in our relationship to Him (forgiveness).

The Jewish people believed that a day was coming when the Messiah would arrive and their sins would be forgiven. There was a time in their history when they were defeated as a kingdom, and taken into captivity. They were taken because of their rebellion against God and sin as a nation. God had promised that even though He had sent them into captivity and suffering, He would not forget about his covenant with them.

God had promised that forgiveness would come when the Messiah came. The Messiah would deliver them from captivity and bring God's healing and forgiveness. When Jesus healed and forgave sins, the Jewish people who believed in him understood that the time of captivity was over. Jesus was showing them that the "day of the Lord" had come; God was offering forgiveness and freedom. The day they had been waiting for was finally here.

REFLECTION ❖

Try to remember a day that you were really excited about. As the day came closer, how did you feel?

How do you think a Jewish person felt as they waited for the day when the Messiah would come and their captivity would be over?

God has promised you a special day that has yet to come. Read the following verses about that day, and write down anything that strikes you in the space below each verse.

Revelation 21:1-6

Revelation 22:1-5

I Peter 1:3-12

I Thessalonians 4:13-18

DAY 11

HEALING IN HIS WINGS

PRAYER ⚬⚬⚬

God, you are called
Jehovah-Mekaddishkem,
the Lord our Sanctifier.
You make all things new.

Thank you for giving me a new life.
I want to glorify you with my whole heart.

Take a few minutes of silence. In your own words, ask God to meet you here.

READING ⚬⚬⚬

Jesus went with him, and all the people followed, crowding around him. A woman in the crowd had suffered for twelve years with constant bleeding. She had suffered a great deal from many doctors, and over the years she had spent everything she had to pay them, but she had gotten no better. In fact, she had gotten worse. She had heard about Jesus, so she came up behind him through the crowd and touched his robe. For she thought to herself, "If I can just touch his robe, I will be healed." Immediately the bleeding stopped, and she could feel in her body that she had been healed of her terrible condition.

Jesus realized at once that healing power had gone out from him, so he turned around in the crowd and asked, "Who touched my robe?"

His disciples said to him, "Look at this crowd pressing around you. How can you ask, 'Who touched me?'"

But he kept on looking around to see who had done it. Then the frightened woman, trembling at the realization of what had happened to her, came and fell to her knees in front of him and told him what she had done. And he said to her, "Daughter, your faith has made you well. Go in peace. Your suffering is over."
—MARK 5:24-34

RESPONSE ⠿

After reading those verses, what are your first impressions? If you were that woman, would you have had enough faith to expect healing by touching his robe? Write down anything that comes to your mind about this passage.

As the woman in this story approached Jesus, he was actually on his way to see someone else who was sick and in need of healing. Desperate for her own pain and bleeding to end, she reached out with faith, believing that touching the fringe of his clothing could bring healing.

Jesus was referred to as a teacher and rabbi by the Jewish people of his day. The normal custom of a rabbi was to wear the traditional priestly garments that included a prayer shawl around the neck. At the end of a traditional prayer shawl are fringes, called "tsi tsi." There is a prophesy in the Old Testament that said the Messiah would come with "healing in his wings." The Hebrew word for wings can also be translated "tsi tsi" or fringes. The Jewish people believed that the Messiah would come with "healing in his fringes." As this woman reached out for the corner of his garment she may have been reaching out in belief that Jesus was the promised Messiah.

In the story, after she touched him, Jesus sensed that healing power had left him. With a huge crowd around him he took time to find out who had reached out in faith to him. He tenderly told her to go in peace—something she had not experienced in a long time.

REFLECTION ❖

Write about a time that you reached out to God in faith. What were you in need of at that time? How did God respond?

Draw a picture of what "healing in his wings" might look like to you. What would the wings of Jesus provide for you?

DAY ELEVEN: HEALING IN HIS WINGS

DAY 12

JESUS AS A PROPHET

PRAYER

Jesus, you were a carpenter,
but you were also Jehovah-Eloheenu,
the Lord our God.

Thank you for being my God.
Speak truth into my life through your word.

Take a few minutes of silence. In your own words, ask God to meet
you here.

READING

Jesus left that part of the country and returned with his
disciples to Nazareth, his hometown. The next Sabbath
he began teaching in the synagogue, and many who
heard him were amazed. They asked, "Where did he
get all this wisdom and the power to perform such
miracles?" Then they scoffed, "He's just a carpenter,

the son of Mary and the brother of James, Joseph, Judas, and Simon. And his sisters live right here among us." They were deeply offended and refused to believe in him.

Then Jesus told them, "A prophet is honored everywhere except in his own hometown and among his relatives and his own family." And because of their unbelief, he couldn't do any miracles among them except to place his hands on a few sick people and heal them. And he was amazed at their unbelief.

Then Jesus went from village to village, teaching the people.
—MARK 6:1-6

RESPONSE

After reading those verses, what are your first impressions? Why do you think Jesus said "a prophet is honored everywhere except in his own hometown . . . ?" Write down anything that comes to your mind about this passage.

INSIGHT

In this passage Jesus refers to himself as a prophet. In the Bible, prophets played an important role for the nation of Israel. Whenever God's people would forget about him and begin living in their own ways, God would send a messenger, or a prophet, to correct them.

In your Bible, read the first chapter of 2 Kings. Notice the warning that Elijah gave for the king. Usually the prophet would warn the people that if they didn't change, bad things were coming.

Sometimes when people were hurting and suffering, a prophet would remind them that they were God's special people and that they would not be forgotten. Read Isaiah 40:1-2.

Most of the prophets in Israel had difficult lives; they were often disliked and rejected for what they said. Because of human nature, people don't like to be corrected—especially by someone who seems like their equal.

In this story, Jesus helped only a few people because of the town's response to him. These people could not get past the fact that Jesus was one of them.

The Bible doesn't say much about Jesus growing up; sometimes people think he was a super-child. But it seems from this story that the people he grew up with thought of him as normal, which is why they had a hard time believing he could be anything more. They could not conceive that he could be a prophet.

REFLECTION

When you think of Jesus as a prophet, in what ways has he corrected and warned you?

In what ways has Jesus encouraged you when you were suffering?

Spend the next few minutes thanking Jesus for being a prophet to you. Write a prayer that expresses your desire to recognize him as a prophet in your life.

DAY 13

THE "IN BETWEEN" WORLD

PRAYER

Jehovah-Shalom, you are
the Lord of Peace.

Bring peace to my world,
and help me to extend
your love and peace to those around me.

Take a few minutes of silence. In your own words, ask God to meet you here.

READING

After they had crossed the lake, they landed at Gennesaret. They brought the boat to shore and climbed out. The people recognized Jesus at once, and they ran throughout the whole area, carrying sick people on mats to wherever they heard he was. Wherever he went—in villages, cities, or the countryside—they brought the sick out to the marketplaces. They begged him to let the sick touch at least the fringe of his robe, and all who touched him were healed.

—Mark 6:53-56

RESPONSE :ᐳ

After reading those verses, what are your first impressions? How do you think the people "recognized Jesus at once?" Write down anything that comes to your mind about this passage.

INSIGHT ⚬

Although Jesus had often asked people he'd healed to keep quiet about it, the news spread that he could perform miracles. In this story people who had heard about Jesus brought their sick friends and family to Jesus with the anticipation that He could change them.

Healing and miracles were a regular part of Jesus' ministry. It was a tangible way for him to demonstrate that the old world of sickness, death, and war is giving way to a new world of healing, wholeness, and peace.

Today we live in the "in between" world. The Kingdom of God is here, but not fully. For now, Jesus calls us to continue his work by the power of the Holy Spirit, bringing wholeness and restoration to everything that we find is broken.

REFLECTION ⚬

Take a few minutes to think about the neighborhood you live in. What is it like?

Does your neighborhood demonstrate brokenness? Make a list of the "broken" things you see in your neighborhood.

For each of these "broken" things, think of a way you could help bring restoration and healing, to help reveal the full Kingdom of God.

This week try out one or two of your ideas.

DAY 14

JESUS CROSSES THE LINES

PRAYER

Jesus, you are the prince of peace.
Pour over me today with
your peace and love.

Remind me of your truth
as I walk through my day.

Take a few minutes of silence. In your own words, ask God to meet you here.

READING

Jesus left Tyre and went up to Sidon before going back to the Sea of Galilee and the region of the Ten Towns. A deaf man with a speech impediment was brought to him, and the people begged Jesus to lay his hands on the man to heal him.

Jesus led him away from the crowd so they could be alone. He put his fingers into the man's ears. Then, spitting on his own fingers, he touched the man's tongue. Looking up to heaven, he sighed and said, "Ephphatha," which means, "Be opened!" Instantly the man could hear perfectly, and his tongue was freed so he could speak plainly!

Jesus told the crowd not to tell anyone, but the more he told them not to, the more they spread the news. They were completely amazed and said again and again, "Everything he does is wonderful. He even makes the deaf to hear and gives speech to those who cannot speak."
—MARK 7:31-37

RESPONSE ⚬⚬

After reading those verses, what are your first impressions? Why do you think Jesus keeps telling people not to talk about the healings? Write down anything that comes to your mind about this passage.

INSIGHT ✿

It might seem strange to us that Jesus would put his fingers in the deaf man's ears, and then spit on his own fingers before touching the man's tongue. But in Jesus' time, healing was a hands-on experience. Just as a doctor today would use an otoscope and a tongue depressor, Jesus was showing the man through his actions that he was going to be healed. Remember, the man couldn't hear, so Jesus couldn't just tell him what was going to happen—he had to show him.

This miracles serves as a symbol for the spiritual deafness that many of us experience from time to time. With our music, TV, and cell phones within our reach most of the time, it's easy to miss what God is trying to say to us. Our ears are clogged with the noise we fill them with, and we become deaf to the still, small voice of God. Like the deaf man, we need Jesus' touch to open our ears again so we can hear God speaking to us.

REFLECTION ✿

What do you find filling your ears more than God's voice?

What could you do to unplug your ears and listen for God?

When you're quiet enough to hear God, what do you hope you'll hear from him?

Spend the next few minutes in complete silence. Try to get rid of anything that may distract you from hearing God's voice. Write down some thoughts to God, and sit quietly for at least five minutes to listen for his response.

DAY 15

JESUS AND HIS SECRETS

PRAYER

Lord Jesus,
fill me with your Spirit
so I can love and serve you
in all that I do.

Open my eyes to see your truth,
and open my heart to love others.

Take a few minutes of silence. In your own words, ask God to meet
you here.

When they arrived at Bethsaida, some people brought a blind man to Jesus, and they begged him to touch the man and heal him. Jesus took the blind man by the hand and led him out of the village. Then, spitting on the man's eyes, he laid his hands on him and asked, "Can you see anything now?"

The man looked around. "Yes," he said, "I see people, but I can't see them very clearly. They look like trees walking around."

Then Jesus placed his hands on the man's eyes again, and his eyes were opened. His sight was completely restored, and he could see everything clearly. Jesus sent him away, saying, "Don't go back into the village on your way home."
—MARK 8:22-26

RESPONSE

After reading those verses, what are your first impressions? Why do you think Jesus had to touch the man's eyes twice to restore his sight completely? Write down anything that comes to your mind about this passage.

This isn't the first time we've heard Jesus tell the people he healed to keep it a secret. Many people wonder why he said this so many times—especially about something so amazing and life-changing.

Take your Bible and read Matthew 13:11-17. After reading Jesus' words in that passage, it might make sense that Jesus wanted to keep his miracles a secret because people weren't ready to hear the truth—or at least understand it. It gives us a glimpse at the bigger picture Jesus was trying to paint: he wanted people to be ready to hear the good news he came to share, and he knew their hearts needed some preparation in order to fully grasp his purpose on earth.

REFLECTION ❖

What is something that God has done in your life that you've wanted to share with everyone?

What do you need to do in your own heart in order to better hear the message Jesus wants to share with you?

Often Jesus will talk about having "ears to hear" and "eyes to see" God's Kingdom. Write a prayer to God, asking him to help you have the ears and eyes needed to really recognize what he is doing around you.

DAY 16

GOD REVEALED THROUGH LUKE

PRAYER

God, author of life,
continue to open my eyes and ears
to the truth in your word.

Help me to learn from Luke
as I enter in to the stories he wrote.
Teach me the lessons that transcend time
and mold me to be more like you.

Take a few minutes of silence. In your own words, ask God to meet you here.

Many people have set out to write accounts about the events that have been fulfilled among us. They used the eyewitness reports circulating among us from the early disciples. Having carefully investigated everything from the beginning, I also have decided to write a careful account for you, most honorable Theophilus, so you can be certain of the truth of everything you were taught.

—LUKE 1:1-4

RESPONSE ⠾

After reading those verses, what are your first impressions? Why do you think Luke "carefully investigated everything" and wrote it all down? Write down anything that comes to your mind about this passage.

INSIGHT

Luke wrote this account of Jesus' life and ministry. The purpose of the book is to write out an orderly account of Jesus' life so that Christians could deepen their faith by being certain of the things they had been taught.

Remember, before the Scriptures were written, they were handed down from generation to generation through oral stories. It would be easy for people to question the authenticity of some of these stories, which is why Luke wrote it all down as a historical account.

REFLECTION

How important is it for you to "be certain of the truth of everything you were taught?" In other words, how much proof do you need in order to believe what you've been told about God?

Take a few minutes to write out your own story. Write the "Gospel According to You" about your journey with Jesus. (You may need more space than is on this page. Feel free to spend more time on this on a separate piece of paper.)

DAY 17

JESUS STANDS AGAINST EVIL

PRAYER

God Almighty,
You are powerful and loving.

I'm grateful for your power in my life.
Help me to walk towards you and away from evil.
Guide me and speak to me
through the miracles of your Son.

Take a few minutes of silence. In your own words, ask God to meet you here.

READING

Once when he was in the synagogue, a man possessed by a demon—an evil spirit—began shouting at Jesus, "Go away! Why are you interfering with us, Jesus of Nazareth? Have you come to destroy us? I know who you are—the Holy One sent from God!"

Jesus cut him short. "Be quiet! Come out of the man," he ordered. At that, the demon threw the man to the floor as the crowd watched; then it came out of him without hurting him further.

Amazed, the people exclaimed, "What authority and power this man's words possess! Even evil spirits obey him, and they flee at his command!" The news about Jesus spread through every village in the entire region.
—LUKE 4:33-37

RESPONSE

After reading those verses, what are your first impressions? How do you think the evil spirit recognized Jesus and his power? Write down anything that comes to your mind about this passage.

INSIGHT

The book of Luke mentions demons twenty-three times, which reveals the big picture of the "good vs. evil" that was taking place then. It's interesting to note that so many people did not yet see who Jesus really was, and yet, this demon recognized him, calling him "Jesus of Nazareth" and "the Holy One sent from God." By naming Jesus, the demon shows the people how significant this battle really was.

The demon asks Jesus if he is going to destroy them. It's hard to know if the demon meant all demons or just him and the man he had possessed. If he meant all demons, it shows that the demon was aware of the power and authority Jesus had over all evil spirits. If he meant himself and the man, it shows that the demon thought he had great control over the man—so much that Jesus could not destroy the demon without destroying the man. It really seems like a challenge to Jesus, who takes it on and destroys the demon without harming the man.

Over and over, God's Word shows that evil can't stand up to righteousness when righteousness stands strong.

REFLECTION

Why do you think the demon asks Jesus if He is going to destroy them?

In what way does this scene represent the way Jesus and Satan are both at work in our world, even today?

How can you "stand strong in righteousness?" What does that mean to you? Read Psalm 121 and write your thoughts about that passage.

DAY 18

JESUS AND THE OFFICER

PRAYER

I have faith in you God,
because you are Jehovah-Shammah,
the present Lord.

I am confident that you are here with me,
speaking to me through your Word.
Deepen my faith today as I grow closer to you.

Take a few minutes of silence. In your own words, ask God to meet you here.

When Jesus had finished saying all this to the people, he returned to Capernaum. At that time the highly valued slave of a Roman officer was sick and near death. When the officer heard about Jesus, he sent some respected Jewish elders to ask him to come and heal his slave. So they earnestly begged Jesus to help the man. "If anyone deserves your help, he does," they said, "for he loves the Jewish people and even built a synagogue for us."

So Jesus went with them. But just before they arrived at the house, the officer sent some friends to say, "Lord, don't trouble yourself by coming to my home, for I am not worthy of such an honor. I am not even worthy to come and meet you. Just say the word from where you are, and my servant will be healed. I know this because I am under the authority of my superior officers, and I have authority over my soldiers. I only need to say, 'Go,' and they go, or 'Come,' and they come. And if I say to my slaves, 'Do this,' they do it."

When Jesus heard this, he was amazed. Turning to the crowd that was following him, he said, "I tell you, I haven't seen faith like this in all Israel!" And when the officer's friends returned to his house, they found the slave completely healed.

—Luke 7:1-10

RESPONSE

After reading those verses, what are your first impressions? Why do you think the officer trusted that Jesus could heal his servant, even if he didn't go to the house? Write down anything that comes to your mind about this passage.

The officer we find in this story is unique in many ways. It was not normal for a Roman officer to love the nation of Israel, or help build synagogues, and an officer was typically not so caring for his servants (who were considered slaves). He stood out to the Jewish elders as someone Jesus should help.

The officer also addresses Jesus as Lord. This is a term of royalty, as in King or master. The Roman citizens of his day would have reserved that title for Caesar only. In fact, on some of the Roman coins of this time Caesar is called the son of god. But this officer addresses Jesus as Lord, not Caesar. He recognizes that all things are under Jesus' authority in the same way his soldiers are under his authority. This Roman officer honors Jesus more than some of God's own people do.

REFLECTION ⚬

Reread Luke 7:1-10 and compare it with the account in Matthew 8:5-13. What things are different?

Why do you think the officer had such a strong faith in Jesus?

In what ways is it obvious to others that you have faith?

How can you demonstrate your faith to those around you? Make a list, and choose one of those things to do this week.

DAY 19

JESUS IN A STRANGE SITUATION

PRAYER

God of peace,
thank you for calming me
in my sometimes chaotic world.

Help me to focus on you today
and to witness your love around me.

Take a few minutes of silence. In your own words, ask God to meet you here.

So they arrived in the region of the Gerasenes, across the lake from Galilee. As Jesus was climbing out of the boat, a man who was possessed by demons came out to meet him. For a long time he had been homeless and naked, living in a cemetery outside the town.

As soon as he saw Jesus, he shrieked and fell down in front of him. Then he screamed, "Why are you interfering with me, Jesus, Son of the Most High God? Please, I beg you, don't torture me!" For Jesus had already commanded the evil spirit to come out of him. This spirit had often taken control of the man. Even when he was placed under guard and put in chains and shackles, he simply broke them and rushed out into the wilderness, completely under the demon's power.

Jesus demanded, "What is your name?"

"Legion," he replied, for he was filled with many demons. The demons kept begging Jesus not to send them into the bottomless pit.

There happened to be a large herd of pigs feeding on the hillside nearby, and the demons begged him to let them enter into the pigs.

So Jesus gave them permission. Then the demons came out of the man and entered the pigs, and the entire herd plunged down the steep hillside into the lake and drowned.

When the herdsmen saw it, they fled to the nearby town and the surrounding countryside, spreading the news as they ran. People rushed out to see what had happened. A crowd soon gathered around Jesus, and they saw the man who had been freed from the demons. He was sitting at Jesus' feet, fully clothed and perfectly sane, and they were all afraid. Then those who had seen what happened told the others how the demon-possessed man had been healed. And all the people in the region of the Gerasenes begged Jesus to go away and leave them alone, for a great wave of fear swept over them.

So Jesus returned to the boat and left, crossing back to the other side of the lake. The man who had been freed from the demons begged to go with him. But Jesus sent him home, saying, "No, go back to your family, and tell them everything God has done for you." So he went all through the town proclaiming the great things Jesus had done for him.

—Luke 8:26-39

RESPONSE

After reading those verses, what are your first impressions? What seemed like the strangest part of the story to you? Write down anything that comes to your mind about this passage.

INSIGHT ⚫⚪

This might be one of the strangest stories in the Gospels. A naked man is talking to Jesus; a herd of pigs runs off a cliff…it's an easy story to imagine in your mind because of the vivid details.

One thing a Jewish person would notice right away in this scene is that it is very "unclean." There were very specific Jewish laws in the Old Testament that gave instructions about clean and unclean things. Almost everything in this story is unclean: Gerasenes is mainly a Gentile area, therefore considered to be unclean, as were cemeteries, demons, and pigs. Jesus, as a Jewish teacher, should be far away from all unclean things, and here he is in the middle of it.

Jesus said in the beginning of his ministry that he was going to bring freedom to captives, sight to the blind, and that the downtrodden will see freedom and wholeness. In this story the naked, possessed man ends up clothed and healed, sitting at Jesus' feet. This story shows Jesus entering into our unclean-ness, and bringing wholeness.

REFLECTION ⚫⚫

In your Bible, read Matthew 15:10-20. In light of this passage, think about things that make you unclean. Write them down, and as they come to your mind, ask Jesus to make you clean and whole like he did for the man in the story.

Write a prayer thanking God for making it possible for you to be clean.

DAY 20

JESUS CONQUERS DEATH

PRAYER

God of Life,
you have conquered death.
You've rescued me from eternal death
and welcomed me into your family.

Calm my fears and strengthen my faith
through your power and love.

Take a few minutes of silence. In your own words, ask God to meet you here.

On the other side of the lake the crowds welcomed Jesus, because they had been waiting for him. Then a man named Jairus, a leader of the local synagogue, came and fell at Jesus' feet, pleading with him to come home with him. His only daughter, who was about twelve years old, was dying...

While he was still speaking to her, a messenger arrived from the home of Jairus, the leader of the synagogue. He told him, "Your daughter is dead. There's no use troubling the Teacher now."

But when Jesus heard what had happened, he said to Jairus, "Don't be afraid. Just have faith, and she will be healed."

When they arrived at the house, Jesus wouldn't let anyone go in with him except Peter, John, James, and the little girl's father and mother. The house was filled with people weeping and wailing, but he said, "Stop the weeping! She isn't dead; she's only asleep."

But the crowd laughed at him because they all knew she had died. Then Jesus took her by the hand and said in a loud voice, "My child, get up!" And at that moment her life returned, and she immediately stood up! Then Jesus told them to give her something to eat. Her parents were overwhelmed, but Jesus insisted that they not tell anyone what had happened.
—LUKE 8:40-42A, 49-56

RESPONSE

After reading those verses, what are your first impressions? How do you think the parents felt after seeing their daughter die and come back to life? Write down anything that comes to your mind about this passage.

INSIGHT ✿

Up to this point, we've only looked at miracles that Jesus performed on living people. This time we see him bring someone back to life after they've been dead. Even though Jesus says she is only sleeping, it's obvious that she had been dead, because the crowd of mourners would only arrive after hearing that someone had died. This miracle shows us the power that Jesus has over death—and as we'll later witness, even over his own death.

The fear of death is a common fear for most people. For us, death is often difficult to face, or even be around, because we feel so powerless. Death feels so final. But it's important to remember the life after death that Jesus has promised, and the power that he has to bring us to that life.

REFLECTION ✿

What is something you fear?

On a scale of one to ten how much of a fearful person are you? (One being not at all, ten being totally scared.)

In your Bible, read Matthew 6:25-33. Take a moment to think about the things that are causing you to worry now. One by one let them rise up to God as you ask him to care for your fears. If it helps you to visualize it, draw a fire and write your fears in the smoke rising from the fire.

DAY 21

JESUS HEALS TEN LEPERS

PRAYER

Father God, maker of all,
Thank you for today.
Help me to live today like you want me to;
to love and serve those around me.

Give me grace for those who are different
And love for people who are hard to love.

Take a few minutes of silence. In your own words, ask God to meet you here.

As Jesus continued on toward Jerusalem, he reached the border between Galilee and Samaria. As he entered a village there, ten lepers stood at a distance, crying out, "Jesus, Master, have mercy on us!"

He looked at them and said, "Go show yourselves to the priests." And as they went, they were cleansed of their leprosy.

One of them, when he saw that he was healed, came back to Jesus, shouting, "Praise God!" He fell to the ground at Jesus' feet, thanking him for what he had done. This man was a Samaritan.

Jesus asked, "Didn't I heal ten men? Where are the other nine? Has no one returned to give glory to God except this foreigner?" And Jesus said to the man, "Stand up and go. Your faith has healed you."
—Luke 17:11-19

RESPONSE ⦙⦙

After reading those verses, what are your first impressions? Why do you think the other nine men did not return to praise Jesus? Write down anything that comes to your mind about this passage.

INSIGHT

You may remember from earlier devotions that many Jewish people considered Gentiles unclean. There was another group of people that caused tension among many Jewish people—the Samaritans. The Samaritans were part Jewish and part Gentile, and therefore were considered unclean by many of the Jewish people.

In this story, the fact that the only person who came back after being healed by Jesus was the Samaritan made the Jewish people look bad. It only added to the anger the Jewish leaders had towards Jesus when they would hear stories like this. But it showed God's love for all people—that Jesus would heal both Jewish people and Samaritans.

REFLECTION

Who are considered to be the Samaritans or Gentiles in our society today? In other words, what kinds of people do some Christians think are not loved by God?

How do you feel about people who are different from you—or are not followers of Jesus?

This week, think about the fact that Jesus hung around with the people who were rejected by others—and he was criticized for it. Do something to include someone that may be rejected in your world, even if it means you'll be criticized.

DAY 22

JESUS LOVES HIS ENEMIES

PRAYER

God of love,
teach me to love like you.

Soften my heart towards those who hurt me;
lead me in your ways.

Take a few minutes of silence. In your own words, ask God to meet
you here.

READING

But even as Jesus said this, a crowd approached, led by Judas, one of the twelve disciples. Judas walked over to Jesus to greet him with a kiss. But Jesus said, "Judas, would you betray the Son of Man with a kiss?"

When the other disciples saw what was about to happen, they exclaimed, "Lord, should we fight? We brought the swords!" And one of them struck at the high priest's slave, slashing off his right ear.

But Jesus said, "No more of this." And he touched the man's ear and healed him.
—LUKE 22:47-51

RESPONSE

After reading those verses, what are your first impressions? After all their time with Jesus, why do you think the disciples would react that way? Write down anything that comes to your mind about this passage.

INSIGHT ⁙

In this story we see one of Jesus' best friends betray him. If someone close to you has ever betrayed you, you can understand why the other disciples would have gotten so angry. Nobody likes to see others hurt people they care about. But when the other disciples respond in retaliation and violence, Jesus puts a stop to it (and even heals the man who was there to arrest him). After all, he had been teaching everyone to love their enemies, and therefore lived by that same rule.

While Christians are never to hate people, we are aware that people will hate us. Jesus always taught his followers to respond to others in the way that God responded to them. If God has loved you, you must love others. If God has forgiven you, you must forgive others. If God did not strike you, you must never strike others.

Jesus taught that when we love our enemies we live the Gospel. In fact, this was one of the ways early Christians stood out as light in darkness. Imagine what would happen today if a generation of Christians placed an emphasis on loving those who stand in opposition to them.

REFLECTION ⁙

How do you typically respond to your enemies (or to anyone who hurts you)?

How can you show love to those who hurt you? (Sometimes, in cases of abuse, this is one of the hardest questions to answer. If you're in that situation, spend some time praying for God to reveal his love to you, and remind you how precious you are.)

Write a letter to God. Ask him to help you learn to love those who hurt you, and to see those people the way he sees them.

DAY 23

GOD REVEALED THROUGH JOHN

PRAYER

Lord God,
reveal yourself to me through your servant, John.
Help me to experience what he saw
and know Jesus like he did.

Open my eyes
to the truth you want me to see
and give me wisdom to use that truth in my life.

Take a few minutes of silence. In your own words, ask God to meet you here.

READING

The disciples saw Jesus do many other miraculous signs in addition to the ones recorded in this book. But these are written so that you may continue to believe that Jesus is the Messiah, the Son of God, and that by believing in him you will have life by the power of his name.
—JOHN 20:30-31

RESPONSE

After reading those verses, what are your first impressions? How do Jesus' miracles help you believe in him more? Write down anything that comes to your mind about this passage.

INSIGHT ✦

John was one of the disciples. He was Peter's brother, and describes himself as the disciple who Jesus loved. His gospel is different from the other three gospels in a few ways. It is not a synoptic gospel, which means it does not follow a timeline of events like the other three gospels do. John's gospel is full of symbolism and interpretation.

John spends more time developing the relationship between the Father and the Son. His book is the starting point for the idea of the Trinity. His gospel also spends more time describing the relationship between Jesus and the disciples. The phrase "Kingdom of God" is used only twice, and there are no stories about Satan, demons, or demon-possessed people, unlike the other three gospels.

It's because John spends more time focused on these things that he says in the passage above that there are many other miraculous signs that he did not include in his book.

REFLECTION ✦

Why do you think John left out stories about Satan and demons?

Why do you think John spends more time talking about the relationships Jesus had with God and the disciples?

How would you describe your relationship with God?

What can you do to deepen your relationship with God?

DAY 24

JESUS IS KING OF ALL

PRAYER

You are King of kings,
Lord of lords.

I want to serve you more.
Help me to bow down my life to you
and make you my king.

Take a few minutes of silence. In your own words, ask God to meet
you here.

Once more he visited Cana in Galilee, where he had turned the water into wine. And there was a certain royal official whose son lay sick at Capernaum. When this man heard that Jesus had arrived in Galilee from Judea, he went to him and begged him to come and heal his son, who was close to death.

"Unless you people see miraculous signs and wonders," Jesus told him, "you will never believe."

The royal official said, "Sir, come down before my child dies."

Jesus replied, "You may go. Your son will live."

The man took Jesus at his word and departed. While he was still on the way, his servants met him with the news that his boy was living. When he inquired as to the time when his son got better, they said to him, "The fever left him yesterday at the seventh hour."

Then the father realized that this was the exact time at which Jesus had said to him, "Your son will live." So he and all his household believed.
—JOHN 4:46-53 (NIV)

RESPONSE

After reading those verses, what are your first impressions? Why
do you think Jesus healed the boy without even going to see him?
Write down anything that comes to your mind about this passage.

The town of Cana is the location of the first miracle Jesus performed, where he turned water into wine at a wedding. This official heard that Jesus was in town and went to seek him out. Most people believe this official was a Gentile, and some believe this is the Roman officer from the other gospels. Either way it marks a special day, in that Jesus granted healing to a Gentile. Once again, he was revealing to everyone that the message of God becoming King in the form of Jesus was not only for the Jewish people, but also for the whole world.

John also makes a point to note that this person is a royal official. All through the gospels we see powerful people in positions of authority coming to Jesus. Jesus coming as the King means that all other authorities are under His authority, and some of those leaders recognized and regarded him as King.

REFLECTION ⚬⚬

When you think of the way you approach Jesus, do you identify with the people who need to see a sign to believe or the officer who believed even without a sign? Why do you identify with that side?

If Jesus is the King of all things, how have you identified him as your King, or given him leadership in your life?

What areas of your life do you still need to bring under his leadership?

Take a minute and ask the Spirit to point any areas of your life that you are controlling, and as they come to mind talk to God about them. If you are ready to, ask Him to take over leadership of that area. If you are not ready, spend a few minutes writing about why you won't give them up yet.

DAY 25

JESUS HEALS AT THE POOL

PRAYER

You are Jehovah-Ropheka,
the Lord our healer.

Thank you for healing
the places in my life that hurt.
Thank you for giving me
exactly what I need when I need it.

Show me today how I can help to heal others
and introduce them to your healing love.

Take a few minutes of silence. In your own words, ask God to meet you here.

Afterward Jesus returned to Jerusalem for one of the Jewish holy days. Inside the city, near the Sheep Gate, was the pool of Bethesda, with five covered porches. Crowds of sick people—blind, lame, or paralyzed—lay on the porches. One of the men lying there had been sick for thirty-eight years. When Jesus saw him and knew he had been ill for a long time, he asked him, "Would you like to get well?"

"I can't, sir," the sick man said, "for I have no one to put me into the pool when the water bubbles up. Someone else always gets there ahead of me."

Jesus told him, "Stand up, pick up your mat, and walk!"

Instantly, the man was healed! He rolled up his sleeping mat and began walking!
—JOHN 5:1-9A

RESPONSE ⠿

After reading those verses, what are your first impressions? Why do you think the man just lay there waiting for thirty-eight years? Write down anything that comes to your mind about this passage.

INSIGHT

The pool of Bethesda was a place in Jerusalem where sick people gathered in the hope that they might be healed. The belief was that an angel moved the waters at certain times to cure people. Only the first person to enter the water while it was being stirred would be healed. With all of the people gathered around the water, you can imagine it was quite a scene when the water was stirred. Only the strongest and quickest could beat the rush and be healed. For thirty-eight years the man in this story couldn't beat out the others to get into the pool; and no one else would help him.

When someone is in need and they can't get to the help, we see in this story that Jesus brings help to him. The man spent thirty-eight years waiting for someone to help him, and Jesus was the only one who did.

REFLECTION

Imagine that Jesus has walked into the place you are in right now. What would your response be in seeing him? How would you feel? What would you say?

If Jesus asked you, "Do you want to get well?" what area of your life do you think he'd be asking about? What would your answer be?

If your city were Jerusalem, where would you find the pool? Where are people gathered looking for healing and help?

Write down some ways that you could go and show Jesus' heart to the people who have no one to help them. Make a plan to do at least one of those things this week.

DAY 26

JESUS SHOWS WHO'S REALLY BLIND

PRAYER

God, you are the everlasting King
who has welcomed me into your kingdom.

Allow me to see others like you do.
Open my eyes so I can truly see.

Take a few minutes of silence. In your own words, ask God to meet
you here.

READING

As he went along, he saw a man blind from birth. His
disciples asked him, "Rabbi, who sinned, this man or
his parents, that he was born blind?"

"Neither this man nor his parents sinned," said Jesus, "but this happened so that the work of God might be displayed in his life. As long as it is day, we must do the work of him who sent me. Night is coming, when no one can work. While I am in the world, I am the light of the world."

Having said this, he spit on the ground, made some mud with the saliva, and put it on the man's eyes. "Go," he told him, "wash in the Pool of Siloam" (this word means Sent). So the man went and washed, and came home seeing.

His neighbors and those who had formerly seen him begging asked, "Isn't this the same man who used to sit and beg?" Some claimed that he was. Others said, "No, he only looks like him."

But he himself insisted, "I am the man... One thing I do know. I was blind but now I see!"
—JOHN 9:1-9, 25B (NIV)

RESPONSE

After reading those verses, what are your first impressions? Why do you think the disciples assumed his blindness was a result of sin? Write down anything that comes to your mind about this passage.

INSIGHT

During the days of Jesus there was a common religious philosophy that said if you did the right things, life would be good, and if you did the wrong things, life would be bad. This thinking prompted the disciples to ask what specific sin the blind man committed to deserve blindness. Maybe, they thought, his parents had done something bad, so their child was struck with blindness to punish them.

In your Bible, read John 9:35-41. In this passage, Jesus tells the Pharisees that they are worse than blind, because they claim they can see. Their blindness leads to questions like, "Who sinned to make this man blind?" The sin of the Pharisees is judging. They are not interested in helping the blind man, only in judging him. They believed that if he was blind because of sins, he is getting what he deserves.

In another teaching, Jesus tells all of his followers that they are not to judge. They cannot point out a speck out in someone else's eye, because the logs in their own eyes blind them. Jesus can judge because he alone is the one without a log in his eye. He is the only one that can see clearly enough to judge.

REFLECTION

In what ways do you judge other people?

What judgments do you make when you see:

- A homeless person?

- A pregnant teenager?

- Someone who is drunk or high?

- Someone who looks very different than you?

Take some time to ask God to point out people or situations where you might be sinning, by judging. Write out some of your thoughts in a prayer or commitment to live without judging.

DAY 27

JESUS WEEPS OVER LAZARUS

PRAYER

El-Olam, you are the everlasting God.
Thank you for being with me
all the time, and for never leaving me.

Give me strength today to stand for you
and to reveal your love to those around me.

Take a few minutes of silence. In your own words, ask God to meet you here.

READING

When Mary arrived and saw Jesus, she fell at his feet and said, "Lord, if only you had been here, my brother would not have died."

When Jesus saw her weeping and saw the other people wailing with her, a deep anger welled up within him, and he was deeply troubled. "Where have you put him?" he asked them.

They told him, "Lord, come and see." Then Jesus wept. The people who were standing nearby said, "See how much he loved him!" But some said, "This man healed a blind man. Couldn't he have kept Lazarus from dying?"

Jesus was still angry as he arrived at the tomb, a cave with a stone rolled across its entrance. "Roll the stone aside," Jesus told them.

But Martha, the dead man's sister, protested, "Lord, he has been dead for four days. The smell will be terrible."

Jesus responded, "Didn't I tell you that you would see God's glory if you believe?" So they rolled the stone aside. Then Jesus looked up to heaven and said, "Father, thank you for hearing me. You always hear me, but I said it out loud for the sake of all these people standing here, so that they will believe you sent me." Then Jesus shouted, "Lazarus, come out!" And the dead man came out, his hands and feet bound in graveclothes, his face wrapped in a headcloth. Jesus told them, "Unwrap him and let him go!"

Many of the people who were with Mary believed in Jesus when they saw this happen.
—John 11:32-45

RESPONSE ⚬

After reading those verses, what are your first impressions? Why do you think Jesus cried? Write down anything that comes to your mind about this passage.

INSIGHT ⚬

Shortly before Lazarus died, his sisters, Mary and Martha, sent word to Jesus about their brother's illness. Instead of coming right away, Jesus chose to stay for two more days in the area he was in. By the time he finally did arrive, his good friend Lazarus had died, and four days had passed with him sealed in his tomb.

While Jesus is weeping for his friend, the Pharisees and his friends question his timing. They are judging Jesus. One of the areas people struggle with in faith is seeing God's "inactivity" as "unconcern." In this story, although it looks like Jesus was inactive (because he didn't come right away), he is clearly concerned. The "activity" he does just came at a different time than everyone had expected.

Sometimes we struggle with the practice of patience. It's not easy to wait on God, even if we trust that Jesus has the power to act in our lives. But we should not think that just because we don't see God doing anything, that he's unconcerned or inactive. He may just be waiting for his right time, not ours.

What character in the story did you identify with most? Why?

In what ways was God's timing better than man's in this story?

When you think about patience and God's timing, how is this a challenge to you?

Write a prayer about patience, asking God for His help in practicing patience, and lifting up any areas that you are worried about to Him in prayer.

DAY 28

JESUS DEFIES DEATH

PRAYER

God of Life,
you continue to fill me with your love.
Thank you for the life you've given me.

Help me to use my life
to serve others like Jesus did.

Take a few minutes of silence. In your own words, ask God to meet you here.

READING

Then the disciples went back to their homes, but Mary stood outside the tomb crying. As she wept, she bent over to look into the tomb and saw two angels in white, seated where Jesus' body had been, one at the head and the other at the foot.

They asked her, "Woman, why are you crying?"

"They have taken my Lord away," she said, "and I don't know where they have put him." At this, she turned around and saw Jesus standing there, but she did not realize that it was Jesus.

"Woman," he said, "why are you crying? Who is it you are looking for?"

Thinking he was the gardener, she said, "Sir, if you have carried him away, tell me where you have put him, and I will get him."

Jesus said to her, "Mary." She turned toward him and cried out in Aramaic, "Rabboni!" (which means Teacher).

Jesus said, "Do not hold on to me, for I have not yet returned to the Father. Go instead to my brothers and tell them, 'I am returning to my Father and your Father, to my God and your God.' "

Mary Magdalene went to the disciples with the news: "I have seen the Lord!" And she told them that he had said these things to her.
—JOHN 20:10-18 (NIV)

RESPONSE

After reading those verses, what are your first impressions? How would you have responded if you were Mary? Write down anything that comes to your mind about this passage.

INSIGHT

Throughout John's account of the death and burial of Jesus, he is very deliberate about telling us what day of the week it is. To us this may not seem like a big deal, but when a Jewish person hears the days of the week they automatically think of creation. Jesus suffered on the cross on the sixth day of the week, the final day of work in the creation story. Jesus finished his work on the cross, and then lay in the tomb on the Sabbath—he rested. On Sunday, the first day of a new week, Jesus is found alive in a garden. Later that day, he appeared to the disciples and breathed the Holy Spirit into them, much like the way God first breathed life into Adam.

Through Jesus' death, God has made all things new, and began the work of new creation.

As you look at your life now, in what ways do you need to experience new life?

Make a list of the things in your life that feel old or broken and pray for them, one by one.

Spend a few minutes in prayer, asking Jesus to breathe new life into you.

DAY 29

JESUS SAYS "FORGIVE"

PRAYER

You are Jehovah-Tsidkenu,
Lord of Righteousness.

Thank you for forgiving me.
Pour your love into me today
so I can forgive others.

Take a few minutes of silence. In your own words, ask God to meet you here.

READING

That Sunday evening the disciples were meeting behind locked doors because they were afraid of the Jewish leaders. Suddenly, Jesus was standing there among them! "Peace be with you," he said. As he spoke, he showed them the wounds in his hands and his side. They were filled with joy when they saw the Lord! Again he said, "Peace be with you. As the Father has sent me, so I am sending you." Then he breathed on them and said, "Receive the Holy Spirit. If you forgive anyone's sins, they are forgiven. If you do not forgive them, they are not forgiven."

One of the twelve disciples, Thomas (nicknamed the Twin), was not with the others when Jesus came. They told him, "We have seen the Lord!"

But he replied, "I won't believe it unless I see the nail wounds in his hands, put my fingers into them, and place my hand into the wound in his side."

Eight days later the disciples were together again, and this time Thomas was with them. The doors were locked; but suddenly, as before, Jesus was standing among them. "Peace be with you," he said. Then he said to Thomas, "Put your finger here, and look at my hands. Put your hand into the wound in my side. Don't be faithless any longer. Believe!"

"My Lord and my God!" Thomas exclaimed.

Then Jesus told him, "You believe because you have seen me. Blessed are those who believe without seeing me."

The disciples saw Jesus do many other miraculous signs in addition to the ones recorded in this book. But these are written so that you may continue to believe that Jesus is the Messiah, the Son of God, and that by believing in him you will have life by the power of his name.
—JOHN 20:19-31

RESPONSE

After reading those verses, what are your first impressions? How are you like Thomas in his response to the disciples claims about Jesus? Write down anything that comes to your mind about this passage.

INSIGHT

You can probably imagine the surprise of the disciples when Jesus was suddenly standing in the room with them. They had seen him die on the cross, and they saw his body sealed in the grave. But he appeared and showed them his wounds so they would know for sure that it was him.

But Thomas wasn't there for that event. It's not hard to understand why he could not believe what they were saying—it sounded impossible. It wasn't until Thomas was able to see Jesus for himself, and to touch the wounds, that he was able to believe and recognize Jesus as God. Thomas has been referred to as "Doubting Thomas" for years. But if any of us had been there, chances are that we would have doubted as well.

Jesus reappeared after his death to prove that he was, in fact, God. He came to reveal, once again, that he had power over death—and doubt.

When have you doubted God in your life? Write down some of those times and situations.

How did God reveal his truth to you during those times of doubt?

What could you do to trust God more—even if you can't see him or what he is doing in your life?

Write a prayer to God, asking him to help you trust, and to take away your doubts.

DAY 30

GOD REVEALED THROUGH JESUS' MIRACLES

PRAYER

God, you are the Alpha and Omega,
the beginning and the end.

I take comfort knowing that you've always been here
and you always will be here.

Thank you for being with me
every step I take.
Help direct my steps now
so that I may walk in your ways.

Take a few minutes of silence. In your own words, ask God to meet you here.

READING

"People of Israel, listen! God publicly endorsed Jesus the Nazarene by doing powerful miracles, wonders, and signs through him, as you well know."
—Acts 2:22

RESPONSE

After reading that verse, what are your first impressions? What do you think it means that God "publicly endorsed Jesus?" Write down anything that comes to your mind about this passage.

INSIGHT

Just as Peter says to the people of Israel in this passage, God reveals who he is through the miracles performed by Jesus. It was through the power of God that Jesus was able to heal the sick, cast out demons, and raise people from the dead (including himself).

By studying the miracles of Jesus, we grow closer to knowing the powerful God who sent him to earth to die for us. As we get to know this God, we can learn what it means to follow him and to live the life he has called us to live.

REFLECTION

After studying the miracles of Jesus, what have you learned about God's love for his people?

Which miracle stands out to you the most? Why?

How do you think learning from Jesus' miracles can help you to be more like him?

What miracles would you like to see God perform in our world today? In your life?

Spend some time in prayer. Ask God to show you how Jesus' life and miracles can help you live today. Ask God to open your eyes to the miracles that take place around you every day.